Henry Louis Gates Jr.

Corinne J. Naden and Rose Blue

Chicago, Illinois

For information, address the publisher:
Raintree, 100 N. LaSalle, Suite 1200, Chicago, IL 60602

Photo Research by Scott Braut

Printed and bound in China by South China Printing Company.
10 09 08 07 06
10 9 8 7 6 5 4 3 2 1

Library of Congress Cataloging-in-Publication Data:

Naden, Corinne J.
  Henry Louis Gates, Jr. / Corinne J. Naden and Rose Blue.
    p. cm. -- (African-American biographies)
  Includes bibliographical references and index.
  ISBN 1-4109-1041-5 (hc) 1-4109-1121-7 (pb)
  1. Gates, Henry Louis--Juvenile literature. 2. African American scholars--Biography--Juvenile literature. 3. Critics--United States--Biography--Juvenile literature. I. Blue, Rose. II. Title. III. Series: African American biographies (Chicago, Ill.)
  PS29.G28N33 2005
  810.9'896073--dc22

                                        2005004856

Acknowledgments
The publisher would like to thank the following for permission to reproduce photographs:
p. 4 Bud Williams/New York Daily News; p. 6 Manuscripts and Archives, Yale University Library; pp. 8, 15, 20, 22, 28 Bettmann/Corbis; p. 13 Shepard Sherbell/Corbis Saba; p. 25 courtesy West Virginia University; p. 26 Kennan Ward/Corbis; p. 32 Chris Mellor/Lonely Planet Images; p. 33 Keystone/Getty Images; p. 36 courtesy Vintage Books/ Random House; p. 40 Christopher Felver/Corbis; p. 43 From *The Signifying Monkey: A Theory of African-American Literary Criticism* by Henry Louis Gates, Jr., copyright © 1988 by Henry Louis Gates, Jr. Used by permission of Oxford University Press, Inc.; p. 48 Doug Mills/AP Wide World Photo; p. 50 Syracuse Newspapers/The Image Works; p. 56 courtesy Warner Books

Cover photograph: by Christopher Felver/Corbis

Every effort has been made to contact copyright holders of any material reproduced in this book. Any omissions will be rectified in subsequent printings if notice is given to the publisher

Some words are shown in bold, **like this**. You can find out what they mean by looking in the glossary.

Contents

Henry Louis Gates Jr. is seen here in 1999, the same year he was honored by the American Academy of Arts and Letters, an organization that recognizes notable American artists, writers, and composers.

Introduction:
Talking about Race

Henry Louis Gates Jr., calls himself a "race man" because he writes about African Americans. He wants more people to understand and value the contributions African Americans have made to American **literature** and **culture**.

Gates argues that American students mainly study the works of European writers such as William Shakespeare. Although Gates believes such books are important, he also believes that students do not learn enough about the literature of other **ethnic groups**. He wants students to learn from other cultures and other literature. He believes that most American students go through school thinking that European literature is the only literature one needs to know. He is determined to change that thinking.

Shrewsbury, N. J. 07724. Junior Year was spent studying at the Hebrew University in Jerusalem. Hebrew High School teacher in Fairfield, Ct. sophomore and senior years.

Louis S. Gates. Affiliation: Calhoun. Born: Sept. 16, 1950 in Keyser, W. V. Attended: Piedmont High, Piedmont, W. V. Major: History. 5-year B.A. (2); Secretary, BSAY (2); Daily News (3). Future Occupation: Surgeon. Home Address: 69 Erin St., Piedmont, W. V. 26750

This photo of Gates was included in the 1973 Yale University yearbook.

In His Own Words

"I would never want to get rid of Shakespeare or Milton or Virginia Woolf or any of these people. . . . I want to make room for other great writers—writers like Wole Soyinka or Derek Walcott or Toni Morrison or Marquez. . . . That's been a very important battle and it's a battle, quite frankly, that I think we've now won because most major schools . . . now accept the principles and premises of a **multicultural** literary or multicultural historical [set of available courses]. What we're trying to do at Harvard is to create . . . what I hope will be the greatest center of [thought] concerning persons of African descent in the Old World and the New World."

Gates is a talented teacher, writer, and public speaker. He has taught at several major universities and currently runs the African-American studies department at Harvard University.

He has lived in Europe, Africa, and America. He writes about the experiences he has had as an adult, as well as a child growing up during the **civil rights** movement in the 1950s and 1960s.

Gates has a strong personality and receives a lot of attention. Some people say that he is more of a performer than professor. Indeed, he has become somewhat of a celebrity in the education world. He gives speeches all over the country and discusses Africa and the African-American experience on radio and television. He has also written many books and received numerous honors.

However, Henry Gates does not mind being called a showman. It is worth it, he says, if it helps him get his message across. His message is that serious study of African-American **culture** and literature should be part of the American experience.

This paper mill in West Point, Virginia, shown in the mid-1900s, is very similar to the mill in Henry's hometown of Piedmont, West Virginia.

Chapter 1: Childhood

Born in the village of Piedmont, West Virginia, on September 16, 1950, Henry Louis Gates Jr. grew up on a hillside in West Virginia's Allegheny Mountains. His parents were Henry Gates Sr. and Pauline Coleman Gates.

Piedmont was small and only had a population of 2,565 — mostly Italian and Irish **immigrants** and about 350 African Americans. Today, it is even smaller, with a population of about 1,000 people, about one-third of whom are African Americans.

Henry's uncle gave Henry Jr. the nickname "Skipper." He was often called by his nickname. A skipper is the head, or captain, of a ship. Piedmont was a river town, and ships were very important there.

In the early 1950s, life in Piedmont centered around the paper mill. Nearly everyone in the surrounding area worked there.

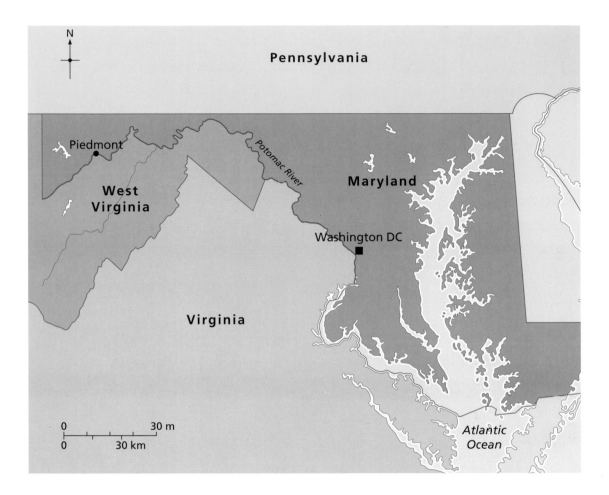

This map shows were Piedmont is located in relation to the surrounding states.

The area was known as the Tri-Towns, consisting of three towns less than a mile apart: Piedmont, West Virginia, and Luke and Westernport in Maryland.

At that time in Piedmont, almost all the African-American mill workers had the same jobs. They also did not have the same opportunity for advancement that white mill workers had. The mill was not **integrated** until 1968. African-American workers were called "loaders" because they spent their days on the shipping platform loading big crates of paper into trucks.

Henry's father was a loader, working six days a week. He started at 6:30 in the morning and worked until the mill whistle blew at 3:30 in the afternoon. School got out at the same time, so Henry hurried home to have dinner at 4 o'clock. His family ate early because his father had to be at his second job at 4:30. Henry's father also worked as a janitor for the telephone company, where he worked until 7:30 in the evening.

At the paper mill, Henry's father also held an important position in the labor union. A labor union is an organization of workers who form a group and work for fair wages and better, safer working conditions.

When Henry was growing up, he and his friends thought there was Piedmont, then everywhere else. They learned about other places through television. Television played a huge role in the Gates household. When Henry's father would come home from work in the evening, the family would gather around the television. Everything they watched would remind their father of something from his past. Gates Sr. would entertain his family with stories.

It was on television that young Henry first learned about Nat King Cole, a jazz singer who was the first African American to have his own television show. Even at a young age Henry understood how important Cole's show was. If Cole's show was successful, it would show the **racists** of the world that they were wrong. It would show them once and for all that African Americans were capable of great achievements. It was also through television that young Henry learned about the **civil rights** movement.

Learning about racism

Henry was aware as a young boy that skin color made a difference. Black people in his town did not eat pizza at the local pizza shop. They did not dance with white people and they certainly did not date them. They could not sit down together and eat at the counter of the local restaurant. Blacks were expected to pick up their food and take it out. They could not even sit down while waiting for it. But Henry's father always sat down. Henry thought it might have been because his father was so light-skinned that the servers at the restaurant could not tell that he was African-American. Or maybe it was just because his father picked up food orders for the telephone workers when he was on his night job, and the restaurant needed the telephone workers' business.

The racism in Piedmont wasn't always as obvious as not being able to eat at the pizza shop. One day in high school, when Henry was walking to school, he fell to the ground in pain. He had

*This photo shows an interracial couple walking in Piedmont, West Virginia, in 1994. Henry Louis Gates grew up in Piedmont in the 1950s and 1960s, before the civil rights movement brought **integration** to American communities.*

injured his hip playing football, and now his hip had come apart. He was rushed to the local hospital and into surgery. There the surgeon, who was white, asked him about his classes. At the time, Henry wanted to be a doctor, so the surgeon asked him a lot of tough science questions. Henry answered them all correctly. He thought the surgeon was testing him to see if he would make a good doctor.

The surgeon decided that nothing was wrong with Henry. He figured Henry was mentally ill. Who ever heard of a black child wanting to be a doctor? The doctor said that the pain in his hip was just part of his mental illness. He made Henry get up from the operating table and try to walk. Henry could not. Fortunately, Henry's mother knew better and took Henry to see someone who could really help him. He ended up in the hospital for six weeks.

U.S. Army troops are pictured in this photo escorting African-American students to classes at Central High School in Little Rock, Arkansas.

Television showed Henry that **racism** was a problem in towns all over the United States. He saw how African Americans in other cities were fighting for fair and equal treatment under the law. News reports that were broadcast on television brought the nation's fight for **civil rights** into their home. When Henry was in second grade, he remembers watching scared young African-American schoolchildren walk into the all-white Central High School in Little Rock, Arkansas. Armed soldiers were there to protect them. White people in Little Rock did not want their school to be **integrated**.

Little Rock, Arkansas, 1957

One of Henry's most frightening childhood memories happened in 1957, when he was in the second grade. Henry still remembers watching television and seeing what happened to nine frightened but brave African-American children in Little Rock, Arkansas.

In 1954 the Supreme Court had ruled that **segregation** in American schools was against the Constitution. But three years later, many schools were still segregated. Orval E. Faubus was the governor of Arkansas in 1957, and he was against **integration.** He thought it should be a local decision, and it was not for the federal government to decide.

But the federal government had decided. In the fall of 1957, nine black students were set to enter Central High School in Little Rock, the state capital. The governor was silent until the night before school opened. Then he made a shocking announcement in a television speech. He said he would order the Arkansas National Guard to prevent the black children from entering the school.

On September 2, the first day of school, the Arkansas National Guard was on duty with their guns ready. They prevented the nine black children from entering Central High. The students were not admitted until September 25, when President Dwight D. Eisenhower sent U.S. Army soldiers to make sure the students were admitted to the school.

Henry himself was one of the first African-American students to attend the newly integrated public schools in Piedmont. This was thanks to a landmark decision by the Supreme Court in a case called *Brown* v. *the Board of Education*. Before the case, black children and white children were forced to go to separate schools. In other words, the schools were segregated. In *Brown* v. *the Board of Education*, the Supreme Court decided that school segregation was illegal.

Henry's parents worked hard to overcome the challenges of **racism**. As a girl, his mother had been a servant for a white family living in a wealthy part of Piedmont. The family had treated her poorly, and Henry's mother grew up distrusting white people. As a boy, realizing this about his mother took Henry by surprise. But the more he heard about his mother's experiences, the more he understood. As adults, Henry and his brother purchased the house where their mother had worked for the white family. Their mother lived there until she died.

While he was still a boy, Henry's mother became the first African-American secretary of the Parent Teacher Association (PTA) in 1957. The PTA is an organization of parents and teachers who work together to make schools better for students. Before Henry's mother became secretary, black women in Piedmont did not join the PTA. But after her election, they began to show up at the meetings. Henry thought they joined just to hear his mother read the notes from the prior meetings in her beautiful, proud voice.

Other lessons learned

Henry credits his parents with his success in life. His parents served as role models. In between watching television and storytelling, the Gates family read. Henry's father did crossword puzzles and was especially fond of detective stories.

Henry's mother worked hard for her family. When Henry was growing up, three of his mother's brothers were in college. They would send Henry's mother their laundry to clean, and she would send it back, pressed and with a bit of money.

One of her brothers, Harry, was so grateful that he wrote in to a television show called *Queen for a Day*. He thought that if anyone should be queen for a day, it was his sister. His letter caught the attention of the people who ran the show and they named Henry's mother queen for a day. She was sent all sorts of glamorous prizes, including clothing, jewelry, and a new set of luggage.

Both of Henry's parents pushed him and his brother Paul Edward to succeed. Their father's two jobs helped put both of his sons through college. Their mother wanted them to dress well, speak well, and go to the very best schools. Henry remembered later, "She wanted us to be as successful as it was humanly possible to be in American society. But she always wanted us to remember that we were black. . . ." Today Henry and his brother believe that their parents lived out all their hopes and dreams through their children.

When Henry reached the fifth grade, he began to learn about Africa. Henry studied a map to find the African countries that he read about. He became fascinated with African geography and history. He remembers, "I busied myself memorizing the names of each African country, their capital, and its leader, pronouncing their names as closely as I could to the way our evening news commentator did on the nightly news."

Discovering James Baldwin

When Henry was twelve, his mother became very sick. The morning she was taken to the hospital, Henry, who had always had a habit of doing things a certain way, decided to change his routine. On this day, instead of crossing his legs left over right, he crossed them right over left. When his mother was taken away, he was sure it was his fault. If only he had stuck to his routine!

Henry made a deal with God. He promised that if his mother was all right, he would join the church. A week later, his mother came back from the hospital. She was not going to die, but she never fully recovered from her illness. Henry kept his promise. He became very religious, and joined the church two weeks later.

Two years later, while he was in the hospital recovering from his hip injury, a local priest named Father Smith drove to the hospital every day to see him. He introduced Henry to many books, including some by the well-known African-American author James

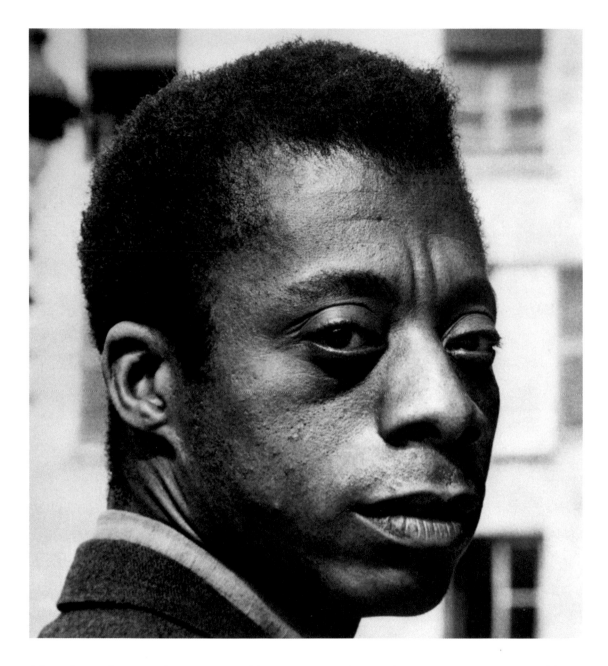

This photo shows author James Baldwin. Henry admired him as a young man. Baldwin inspired Henry to become a writer himself.

Baldwin. Reading Baldwin's books made Gates want to become an **intellectual**.

The next summer, Father Smith gave Henry a copy of Baldwin's book *Notes of the Native Son*, a collection of writings about what it means to be black in the United States. For the first time Henry realized Baldwin was African-American. He fell in love with Baldwin's writing. Suddenly, Henry thought he might want to be a writer himself.

Taking a stand

By the time he was eighteen, Henry had already been active in the fight against **racial discrimination**. In 1968, after Dr. Martin Luther King Jr. was shot and killed, he organized a protest march at his school.

The same year, Henry became involved in trying to **integrate** a local restaurant that held **segregated** dances. The restaurant was called the Swordfish, and it featured live bands on weekends. Henry and three of his buddies walked right into the middle of a whites-only dance one Friday night. A fight started, bottles were thrown, racial slurs were shouted back and forth, and the place was shut down. The police later interviewed the restaurant owner, who called Henry a troublemaker. The owner said he would close down the restaurant before he would open it to blacks. And that is just what happened. The Swordfish was closed and became Samson's Family Restaurant.

*These demonstrators were loaded into a police van in Tennessee after they refused to leave the front of a **segregated** restaurant in 1964. In Piedmont, Gates also protested against such segregation.*

After the restaurant incident, some people in Piedmont began to talk about Henry. They called him names. Remembering the experience later, Henry said that he started to feel as though he were walking around Piedmont with a sign on his back that said he was black and a troublemaker. In fact, he even learned that the county police officers kept a file on him. It made him feel sick and scared.

Henry graduated from high school in 1968. At the top of his class, he gave the **valedictory** speech. He talked about the past twelve years, the Vietnam War that was going on at the time, and the continuing fight for **civil rights**.

After high school graduation, Henry enrolled at Potomac State College, part of West Virginia University. There he began dating a white girl named Maura. They had known each other in high school and met again in college.

People stared at them when they walked on the beach or ate together in a restaurant. Henry had not realized how upset some people could be by the sight of an **interracial** couple. Some people even threatened to hurt him if he continued to date Maura. In time, Henry and Maura went their separate ways.

Changing dreams

Henry went to Potomac State College mostly because it was expected. If you lived in Piedmont and were going to go to college, you went to Potomac. He began to study English and American **literature.** After Potomac, Henry thought he would go on to the university in Morgantown to become a doctor.

But at Potomac, Henry met a man named Duke Anthony Whitmore. Whitmore was a literature teacher, and Henry was one of his students. Henry's cousin had told him to be sure to take Whitmore's literature class.

Henry did take Whitmore's literature class, and many other classes that Whitmore taught. Language and ideas came alive for Henry in those classes. They argued about literature and **racism** and war. At the end of the year, Whitmore urged Henry to go to an Ivy League university instead of to medical school and to think about an **academic** career. Henry agreed, and the decision changed his life.

Gates and Duke Anthony Whitmore met when Gates attended Potomac State College in West Virginia.

This photo shows a village in Tanzania, Africa, near Lake Tanganyika. Gates worked at a hospital in Tanzania between 1970–1971.

Chapter 2:
Learning About Life

In 1969 Gates was accepted at Yale University. He was one of only 95 African-American students accepted at Yale that year. He packed his bag and headed for New Haven, Connecticut.

While at Yale, Henry began to renew the strong interest in African **culture** and **literature** that he had developed in grade school. One of the things he liked most about Yale was the library. There he discovered a huge collection of African-American art and literature. It had been created by Carl Van Vechten, a famous photographer who was very interested in African-American culture. He collected many books on the subject and photographed black artists of the 1920s and 1930s. This was a period of great African-American creativity known as the Harlem Renaissance. Harlem is a thriving black community in New York. "Renaissance" means rebirth.

This photo, taken by Carl Van Vechten, shows poet Countree Cullen. Cullen was one of the leaders of the Harlem Renaissance, a very creative and productive period for many African-American writers, artists, and performers living in New York. Henry Gates currently teaches a course about the Harlem Renaissance at Harvard University.

The Harlem Renaissance

The Harlem Renaissance refers to the period of creativity of African-American artists in the early 20th century. Harlem is a famous district of New York City that has a large African-American community. It has long been known for excellence in music and the arts.

In the 1920s, black musicians, artists, and writers gathered in Harlem to share experiences and encourage each other. They began to experiment in new artistic ways. This coming together stimulated pride and a new confidence in black artistry. Many well-known works resulted from this period. One of them was a collection of poetry by author Langston Hughes called *The Weary Blues.* It appeared in 1926.

The Harlem Renaissance was often helped by grants from organizations. White writers also supported it. However, the Great Depression of the late 1920s and the 1930s caused many of the artists to leave New York or take other jobs.

In the Yale library, Gates also found all kinds of information about the blues, a kind of music he had always loved. Gates wrote a paper about Bessie Smith, the great blues singer, for one of his classes. His professor told him that it was just the kind of thoughtful writing Yale needed in the new field of African-American studies.

Yale allowed Gates to take one year off from his studies. He decided to spend that year in Africa.

To Africa

Henry spent much of the 1970–1971 school year in Tanzania, an African country on the Indian Ocean just south of the equator. It is known for being the home of the tallest mountain in Africa, Mount Kilimanjaro. Henry worked in a hospital in a small village called Kilimatinde. Then, for two-and-a-half months, Gates and a friend hitchhiked from the Indian Ocean to the Atlantic. On the way Gates got very sick. However, he later said that the trip was one of the best experiences of his life.

While in Africa, Gates spent a lot of time learning about different African countries, hiking most of the way and learning about their **cultures.** Gates learned a valuable lesson from the experience. He realized that although his ancestors had come from Africa and although he felt that the culture they brought with them was important, Gates was not an African. He was an American.

Becoming a writer

While in Africa, Gates had written a letter to John J. Rockefeller, a candidate for governor of West Virginia, asking for a job. When he got back to Yale, he found a response waiting for him. He was going to work on Rockefeller's campaign.

Meanwhile, Gates wrote about his experiences in a daily column for the Yale student newspaper, the *Yale Daily News.* His articles got a lot of attention around campus. In one of his classes, his professor complimented a recent article. In that moment, Gates knew he wanted to be a writer. "I was hooked," he remembers.

Instead of taking classes his senior year, the program Gates was in allowed him to write a book. His book, *The Once and Future King,* was about Rockefeller's unsuccessful campaign for governor. It was never published, but his writing was impressive. Henry's adviser at Yale told him that he should be a writer.

In his senior year, Gates won a fellowship to attend Clare College at the University of Cambridge in England. He graduated from Yale with honors in 1973. The next day, he hopped on a ship headed for England. In the meantime, he had sent some of his articles from the *Yale Daily News* and his resume to *Time* magazine. They offered him a job and he wrote for the magazine all summer.

On to Cambridge

By the time he enrolled at Cambridge, Gates had planned to study history. But once he got to the school, Henry focused his studies on **literature.** "I fell in love," he remembers, "not with history, but with the study of English literature."

After Yale, Henry entered Clare College at the University of Cambridge in England.

This change of heart came about in part because of Wole Soyinka, an African playwright who gave guest lectures at Cambridge that year about African **literature**. Gates was Soyinka's only student. "To me he was just a bushy-haired African who wore dashikis [colorful African shirts]," Gates remembers. "I didn't know who he was." Soyinka would later go on to be the first African to win the Nobel Prize in Literature.

Wole Soyinka

Wole Soyinka is considered the most important African writer ever by many people. He is a playwright, a poet, and a novelist. His writing is about the world in which he lives, and much of it is very critical of the government in Nigeria, the country in which he was born. Still, that did not keep him from becoming the first black African to win the Nobel Prize in Literature, which he awarded in 1986.

Soyinka was born on July 13, 1934, in Abeokuta, a town in western Nigeria. He has described his family as "word-spinners" and has said that his mother was full of stories.

In 1964 Soyinka was accused of supporting an antigovernment group and was jailed for 22 months in a cell that was only four feet by eight feet. While imprisoned, Soyinka wrote. He scribbled notes about his prison experience on cigarette package wrappers, toilet paper, in books he read—basically any scrap of paper he could get his hands on. He said later that writing was the only thing that kept him sane. His scribblings became the 1972 book *The Man Died: The Prison Notes of Wole Soyinka.*

Soyinka has lived all over the world and taught at many colleges and universities. And he is still unhappy with the Nigerian government. In 2004, he was in prison again for protesting the government. But not even this has stopped him from writing and standing up for what he believes is right.

Although Soyinka was not given a permanent teaching job at Cambridge (the university was not convinced that there was any real value in studying African **literature**), he became Henry's tutor. He was a strong influence on the direction the young man's career would take. Soyinka also taught Gates a good deal about the Yoruba tribe of West Africa. Henry used much of this knowledge in his later writings.

While studying at Cambridge, Henry also met Kwame Anthony Appiah, a young student from the African country of Ghana. Appiah would later join Henry at Harvard, and then would go on to Princeton University. He would also work with Gates on some of his books. Gates has said that without Wole Soyinka and Kwame Anthony Appiah, he might not have pursued his career and deep interest in African-American studies.

But first Gates really needed to learn to write. The writing he had done for the student newspaper at Yale and for *Time* was not going to be enough if he was really going to be an **intellectual**. He recalls that the first paper he handed in was not well-received by his teacher. "My supervisor said it was the worst essay she ever read." But Gates was determined to improve. He went to a local bookstore and bought book after book about literary criticism. Literary criticism is the term used to describe the process of thinking and writing about writing." I read those books and ended up doing very well," Gates recalls.

Studies and work

Gates earned his master's degree from Cambridge, and then entered the university's doctoral program in English. But after a time, he began to feel limited by the university atmosphere, and he took time off to work at a series of jobs. He continued writing for *Time,* out of the magazine's London office, until 1975. He then returned to the United States and became a public relations representative for the American Cyanamid Company in New Jersey.

During this period of time, he balanced work with his studies. From 1976 to 1979 he was a lecturer at Yale. In 1979, he completed his doctorate work and became the first African American to receive a Ph.D. in English language and literature from Cambridge. Also that year, he married Sharon Adams, a woman he had met while working for Rockefeller in 1971. They would later have two daughters, Maude and Elizabeth.

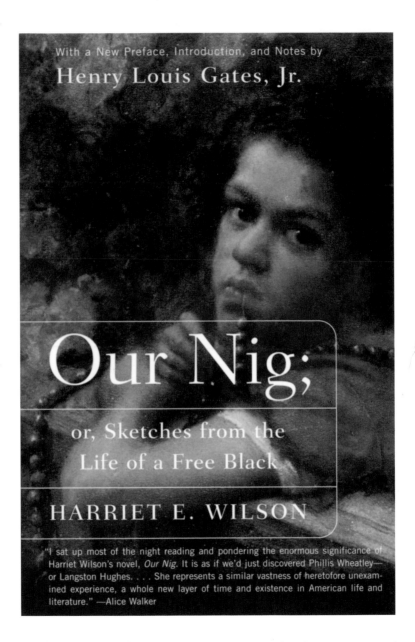

With a New Preface, Introduction, and Notes by
Henry Louis Gates, Jr.

Our Nig;
or, Sketches from the Life of a Free Black

HARRIET E. WILSON

"I sat up most of the night reading and pondering the enormous significance of Harriet Wilson's novel, *Our Nig*. It is as if we'd just discovered Phillis Wheatley— or Langston Hughes. . . . She represents a similar vastness of heretofore unexamined experience, a whole new layer of time and existence in American life and literature." —Alice Walker

With the discovery of Our Nig, *thought to be the first book ever written by a black person and published in the United States, Henry Louis Gates Jr. became something of an **academic** celebrity.*

Chapter 3:
An Important Discovery

In 1979 Gates was invited to teach at Yale. He became an assistant professor of English and the director of a program at Yale in Afro-American studies. ("Afro-American" was a term used at the time.) Henry was determined to build the best African-American **culture** program in the country.

In graduate school, while studying the writings of Africans and African Americans, Gates had become especially interested in works published between the 18th and 20th centuries. Because most blacks in the United States were slaves until the 1850s, few people thought that there had been any significant writing done by blacks during that time. Gates believed otherwise. He knew that what few writings blacks had done during that time were an important part of American history that needed to be studied and celebrated.

Slave narratives

At Yale Gates became determined to uncover documents written by black people. He worked as codirector of the Black Periodical Fiction Project, later renamed the Black Periodical **Literature** Project. Along with Charles T. Davis, who died before the project was finished, Henry collected and described more than 40,000 works written by African Americans. Gates and Davis spent long hours in search of short stories, poems, or almost anything written by or about black Americans. Much of what they found had been lost or forgotten for decades.

Among the writings Gates and Davis collected were slave narratives. These are stories about slavery told by the slaves themselves. Over a period of about 200 years, about 60,000 slaves successfully escaped before slavery ended in 1865. At least 100 of these slaves had written their stories down. These narratives offered important clues about the true horrors of slavery. At the time that Gates was doing his research, the first known slave narrative was *A Narrative of the Uncommon Sufferings and Surprising Deliverance of Briton Hammon, a Negro Man*. It appeared in Boston in 1760.

One day in 1981, Gates was looking through a bookstore in New York City. He discovered a copy of an 1859 novel. It was called *Our Nig; Or, Sketches from the Life of a Free Black, in a Two-Story White House, North: Showing that Slavery's Shadows Fall*

Even There. It was long thought that this book was written by a white man from the North. But Henry did some detective work after finding the novel. He discovered that the author was actually a black woman, Harriet E. Wilson. At that time, Gates determined that Wilson was the first black person to have a book published in the United States. The work had been lost and forgotten for more than a century, but Gates gave the book its proper place in history.

Henry Gates is shown here in a photo from 2000, taken in Boston.

Chapter 4:
The Literary Critic

Henry Gates was becoming very well known for uncovering lost or forgotten literary works. He was also becoming well known as a literary critic—someone who wrote and thought about **literature**. In 1983 Gates wrote an article called "On the Blackness of Blackness," which was about looking at African-American literature as a way to understand African-American history. The next year, Gates published a collection of essays about the literature of black Africans and Americans. It was considered an important contribution to the understanding of black literature.

In 1984 Gates was promoted to associate professor of English at Yale. However, the following year he **resigned** because Yale did not grant him **tenure**. Disappointed, Gates accepted a job as professor of English and African Studies at Cornell University in Ithaca, New York. His friend Kwame Appiah, who had been with him at Yale, soon joined him at Cornell.

Looking at language

Gates' writing career blossomed over the next few years. In 1989 he gained nationwide attention with the publication of *The Signifying Monkey*. The book took Gates ten years to write. *The Signifying Monkey* was inspired by ideas Gates developed through his years of teaching and research about the patterns of African speech.

The Signifying Monkey's title comes from an old African tale about a monkey who teases a lion. The word "signifying" in the book's title refers to a kind of language game in which the meanings of words are twisted and changed to create new meanings. According to Gates, the practice of "signifying" came from slaves. Many slaves did not want to learn the language of their white masters, so they created a language of their own. This helped them send each other secret messages that their masters could not understand.

Gates' new book was very well received. One critic said that Gates showed a new way of looking at the world and its languages. The book earned Gates an American Book Award. The American Book Awards are given each June to honor American writers.

The book The Signifying Monkey *won Gates an American Book Award in 1989. It was honored along with sixteen other books.*

The Tale of the Signifying Monkey

In **cultures** all over the world, trickster characters, or characters who fool and outwit other characters, appear often and in many different forms.

According to Gates, the signifying monkey was first seen in the stories of the Yoruba of Nigeria and other parts of West Africa. There are several variations of the story that involve the characters Monkey, Lion, and Elephant. In all of the stories, Monkey tells Lion that Elephant has insulted Lion. Monkey does this simply to stir up trouble.

Lion approaches Elephant for an apology. Angry at Lion's insult, Elephant (who never insulted Lion to begin with) beats Lion. Lion then realizes that Monkey was lying. The stories end with Lion threatening Monkey and ordering Monkey and his children to stay in the trees.

Many American slaves were from Western Africa and they brought these stories with them. Similar stories can be found in other African cultures, as well as other cultures that were influenced by Africans.

The rap scene

Gates' interest in language got him involved in an **obscenity** trial in 1990. Members of the hip-hop group 2 Live Crew were arrested after they performed at a Florida club in June of that year. They were put on trial for performing songs with obscene lyrics from their album titled *As Nasty as They Wanna Be*. It was the first time that a record in the United States was declared by the law to be obscene.

Columnist George Will wrote in *Newsweek* that the lyrics of the 2 Live Crew album were filthy. But Gates defended the group. He believed their music was not meant to be taken seriously . He testified at the criminal trial, calling the group brilliant artists, and their lyrics a kind of **cultural** expression. Gates said it is impossible to tolerate a culture if it is not understood. 2 Live Crew was eventually found not guilty. "Nothing I've ever done has attracted as much hate mail as my testimony for 2 Live Crew," Gates remembers.

Down South

After five years at Cornell, Gates made another change. Duke University in North Carolina invited him to join the **faculty,** so in 1990 Gates and his wife moved there. He was named the John Spencer Basset Professor of English at the university. But this proved a difficult time for Gates and for his family. Few people were comfortable with the new **interracial** couple in their neighborhood. Gates and his wife found that they experienced more **racism.** Between this and his defense of the rap group 2 Live Crew, Gates was not a popular figure on campus. The student newspaper was critical of him for his part in the trial. Other African Americans on the **faculty** gave him little support.

Harvard calls

Harvard University called Gates in 1991. They wanted him to head an African-American studies department, which was in need of strong leadership. Gates quickly accepted, and his family moved to Massachusetts. Gates became, and continues to be, the W. E. B. DuBois Professor of the Humanities and director of the W. E. B. DuBois Institute for African and African American Research.

Within a few years after his arrival, the enrollment in African-American studies tripled. Gates brought in such lecturers as film director Spike Lee and Wole Soyinka. He hired what he called a "dream team" of black scholars for the department. With these changes came a new respect for the program.

In addition to his work at Harvard, Gates continued to write. Perhaps his best-known work is *Loose Cannons: Notes on the Culture Wars*, published in 1992. He talks about **literature** and **multiculturalism**. He stresses that there must be greater **diversity** in American studies. Gates fears that without the blending of many **cultures**, the original ideals of life and liberty

Spike Lee

One of Gates's guest lecturers in the African-American studies program at Harvard was the well-known film director Spike Lee. His real name is Shelton Jackson Lee, and he was born in Atlanta, Georgia, in 1957. However, he grew up in Brooklyn, New York. His mother was a schoolteacher and his father was a jazz musician. His mother gave him the nickname Spike.

While at Morehouse College in Atlanta, Lee decided to pursue a career in film. He knew that he wanted to direct films, but not just any films. He wanted to direct films that spoke of being African-American. Lee enrolled in the graduate film program at New York University. His first student film, *Joe's Bed-Stuy Barbershop: We Cut Heads*, won the 1983 Academy Award for student films.

From then on, Spike Lee made movies. He was not afraid to face tough issues. His movies looked at violence and racial tension. The 1989 film *Do the Right Thing* was nominated for an Academy Award for best original screenplay. Other films such as *Jungle Fever* and *Mo' Better Blues* established him as a respected director. The film that caused the most controversy for Lee was *Malcolm X*, the story of the famous African-American leader. His 1997 film, a documentary called *4 Little Girls*, was also nominated for an Academy Award. It is the story of the 1963 bombing in Birmingham, Alabama, that killed four African-American girls.

*Gates received the National Humanities Medal in 1998 from U.S. President Bill Clinton. The award is given to individuals or groups each year whose work deepens the nation's understanding of areas of study such as history and **literature**.*

upon which the United States was founded will die. Society cannot survive, he says, without **tolerance** and understanding.

Remembering

While Gates was at an **academic** conference in Italy, he woke up one morning and looked out the window. The Italian countryside reminded him of his hometown of Piedmont, West Virginia. So, he decided to write a book. *Colored People: A Memoir* was dedicated to his parents and published in 1994. He wrote the book especially for his two daughters. He wanted them to know what it was like for him growing up in Piedmont in the 1950s and 1960s. His daughters were growing up in much different circumstances than he did.

Each day, he wrote his daughters a letter, which became the chapters of the book. He described the closeness of his family life, the troubles he ran into, and how African Americans lived in that time and place.

Because of his writings and his academic work, *Time* named Henry Gates as one of the 25 most influential Americans in 1998. *Newsweek* said he was one of the 100 Americans that people should watch in the next century.

Gates is shown in this photo lecturing at Hamilton College in Clinton, New York.

Chapter 5:
The Academic Personality

Gates liked to involve himself in large projects to promote his ideas on race and **literature**. One large project released in 1998 was the *Norton Anthology of African American Literature*. It took ten years to complete with the help of Nellie Y. McKay, a professor of African-American studies at the University of Wisconsin. The book covers 200 years and 2,265 pages. It contains a 1773 poem by Phillis Wheatley, the first black person to publish a poetry book in English. It also covers Toni Morrison, winner of the Nobel Prize in Literature in 1993. In between are 120 other writers, showing the range of black literature in America.

The editors wanted readers to understand the importance of black literature in the fight for freedom and equality in the United States. Gates said that he felt this book was the most important collection of black writings in 250 years of English publications.

Another new idea Gates launched in January 1999 promoted knowledge about Africa and its **culture** through a CD-ROM encyclopedia called *Encarta Africana.* It was edited by Gates and Kwame Appiah. The idea came from a vision by W. E. B. DuBois. DuBois had wanted to create an encyclopedia that would describe the history and culture of black people from all parts of the world. In the early 1970s Gates and Kwame Appiah talked about one day being able to publish such a work.

More than twenty years later, the idea became a reality. After they reached a deal with Microsoft, it took fifteen months to complete the project. Gates and Appiah hired a staff of seventeen writers. When it was published, reviewers said it brought the study of Africa to a new level in the United States.

Gates said that *Encarta Africana,* among other things, gives students an opportunity to "hear how blackness sounds." One way to bring the ideas to life was by including historical audio clips of such early black leaders as Marcus Garvey and Booker T. Washington.

This venture into teaching through new technology provided viewers with information about everything African. A website connected with the project immediately became so popular that Gates had to hire a full-time editor to keep adding articles. Artwork by African Americans also appeared on the site, so did feature stories about black people in the news.

Henry's hero

One of the people Henry Gates respects the most is the man for whom an institute at Harvard is named: W. E. B. (William Edward Burghardt) DuBois (1868–1963). He has been called the most important leader for African Americans in the first half of the 20th century. He helped to create the National Association for the Advancement of Colored People (NAACP) in 1909.

DuBois was born in Massachusetts and graduated from Fisk University, a black college in Tennessee, in 1888. He earned a doctoral degree from Harvard in 1895. He became a professor at Atlanta University in 1897, where he published the first study of a black community in the United States in 1899.

At first, DuBois thought race problems in the United States could be settled peacefully. But he later came to feel that protest was the only answer. Because of this, he had problems with many other black leaders of the time. Over the next several decades, DuBois wrote books on race relations in the United States and continued to teach in Atlanta.

By the early 1950s, DuBois no longer believed that America's race problems could be solved. He moved more and more toward **communism.** He joined the Communist Party in 1961 and moved to Ghana, where he died in 1963.

Gates was able to get grants from foundations. With this money he was able to give the *Encarta Africana* CD-ROM to poor schools in cities with a large black population, such as Washington, D.C.

In 1999 Gates completed still another large project after about a year of filming. This was a television series for public television called *Wonders of the African World*. For six hours, viewers followed Gates as he explored twelve African countries. He introduced the viewer to stories of ancient lands and to all kinds of people from kings to the relatives of slave traders. Viewers saw modern-day Africans at work. They also saw centuries-old civilizations that have been long forgotten by most of the world.

Another discovery

When Gates uncovered the long-forgotten book *Our Nig* in 1981, it was thought to be the first novel known to have been written by a African-American woman. But that changed in 2002 when *The Bondwoman's Narrative* was published.

A year before, Gates saw an ad in an art gallery catalog in New York City. It told of a manuscript handwritten and bound in cloth. It had come from a private collection and might have been written by a slave. The full title was *The Bondwoman's Narrative by Hannah Crafts, a Fugitive Slave, recently escaped from North Carolina.*

Gates bought the manuscript for $8,500. The pages were yellow and faded. He tried to find out when they were written. Experts dated the book to the 1850s.

Gates tried, but could not find any further information about a slave named Hannah Crafts. However, all the places and people she named in the book were real and documented. For instance, she talked of her owner, John Hill Wheeler. Gates discovered he was indeed a slave owner in North Carolina and served as assistant secretary to U.S. President Franklin Pierce.

With the book's publication in 2002, it became the first known novel written by an African-American woman in the United States. It is also the only known handwritten account by a runaway slave.

This photo shows the title page of The Bondwoman's Narrative by Hannah Crafts. Gates edited the manuscript of the book for its 2002 publication.

Chapter 6:
An Idea of Excellence

In January 2002, Harvard University president Lawrence Summers met with professors Cornel West and Henry Gates. Summers had taken over as university president the year before. Word had spread that both scholars were unhappy with the president's leadership. It was said they were both considering going to Princeton University in New Jersey.

The reason for their unhappiness was the African-American studies program. Both men felt that Summers was not doing enough to strengthen and promote it. In the end, Cornel West left the university for Princeton, as did Henry's longtime friend Kwame Appiah, but Gates remained. He said that he believed the new president and administration were serious about the African-American studies program at Harvard. Gates called it a time of rebuilding.

Gates today

Today, Henry Gates is almost better known for what he does outside the university than in it. He is still a college professor at Harvard and continues to teach courses each year. Three of Henry's well-known courses at Harvard are on the tradition of African-American **literature**, writings of African-American women, and the Harlem Renaissance.

In the spotlight

In addition to his teaching, Henry Gates is also a writer, a literary critic, a television speaker, a discoverer of rare literature, and a friend of the rich and powerful. He counts as his friends former U.S. President Bill Clinton, Bill Gates of Microsoft, and many others celebrities. He writes articles for television and for the *New Yorker* magazine. He was an adviser when former U.S. Vice President Al Gore ran for president in 2000. He delivers speeches to colleges, universities, and other groups all over the country. Some believe he is the top expert on all things African-American.

Henry Gates has become well known as a result of his endless work to expose African and African-American literature, culture, and history to the world. The author of numerous books and articles, he has more than 40 **honorary degrees** and other awards. But no matter what he is involved in, Gates says his main concern is African-American studies. His dream is that there will

will one day be several great centers for African-American learning in the United States. He continues to work toward this goal.

In His Own Words

"Among the people I like to think of as useful role models are author-educator W. E. B. DuBois, **civil rights activist** Mary Church Terrell, Nigerian playwright Wole Soyinka, South African leader Nelson Mandela, novelist Toni Morrison, and poet Phillis Wheatley. She learned English when she was about seven, and by the age of fifteen she was publishing poems as sophisticated as any American who was publishing in the 18th century. We need to make that common knowledge, as common as the fact that Michael Jordan can do the triple, quadruple, backward dunk."

Glossary

academic referring to school or college

activist person who believes in taking forceful action for political purposes

civil rights rights of all United States citizens to fair and equal treatment under the law. The civil rights movement was the name given to the long fight to gain civil rights for African Americans.

communism system of government in which all property is owned by the government and all people have an equal share of the land and businesses. A communist is a person who believes in communism.

culture knowledge, beliefs, and behavior of a group of people

discrimination treatment of some people better than others without a proper or fair reason

diversity condition of being different

ethnic group group of people who share a common race, language, and culture

faculty teachers in a school or university

honorary degree honor given by a university to a person the university feels has demonstrated a commitment to learning

immigrant person who moves to a new country to live there

integrate bring groups together, such as white and black people

intellectual person engaged in learning and thinking

interracial relating to, or involving people of different races

literature written works having lasting interest and ideas

multicultural relating to or including many cultures

obscenity language or action considered unacceptable; swear word

racism belief that people of different races are not as good or equal as others. A racist is a person who practices racism.

resign quit

segregate to separate, by races for example

tenure promotion given to university professors guaranteeing their right to their jobs. A tenured professor is very difficult to fire.

tolerance ability to accept others' feelings and ideas that are different from one's own

valedictory closing or farewell statement, especially at a graduation

Timeline

1950 Henry Louis Gates Jr. is born in Piedmont, West Virginia, on September 16.

1968 Gates tries to **integrate** a restaurant in his hometown, graduates from high school, and enrolls at Potomac State College.

1969 Gates enters Yale University.

1973 Selected as Yale Scholar of the House.

1973 Graduates from Yale and enters Clare College at the University of Cambridge.

1974–1979 Lectures at Yale, earns degrees from Cambridge, marries Sharon Adams, and joins Yale **faculty**.

1981 Recovers "lost" 1859 novel and receives genius award from MacArthur Foundation.

1984 Publishes *Black Literature and Literary Theory* and is promoted to associate professor of English and African studies.

1985 **Resigns** from Yale and joins Cornell University.

1989 Publishes *The Signifying Monkey*.

1990 Testifies at 2 Live Crew **obscenity** trial.

1991 Heads African-American studies department at Harvard University and becomes director of W. E. B. Du Bois Institute for African and African-American Research.

1998 Named one of *Time* magazine's most influential Americans and completes *Norton Anthology of African American Literature* with Nellie Y. McKay.

1998 Edits CD-ROM encyclopedia *Encarta Africana* with Kwame Appiah and completes TV series *Wonders of the African World*.

Further Information

Further reading

Howard, Melanie A. *Civil Rights Marches*. Edina, Minn.: ABDO Publishing, 2004.

Kjelle, Marylou Morano. *Henry Louis Gates, Jr*. Philadelphia: Chelsea House, 2004.

Worth, Richard. *Slave Life on the Plantation: Prisons Beneath the Sun*. Berkeley Heights, N.J.: Enslow Publishers, 2004.

Addresses

Henry Louis Gates Jr.
W. E. B. Du Bois Institute
Harvard University
Barker Center
12 Quincy Street
Cambridge, MA 02138

Institute for African American Studies
312 Holmes
Hunter Academic Building
University of Georgia
Athens, GA 30602

Black Men of America
141 Auburn Avenue
Atlanta, GA 30303

National Association of Equal Opportunity and Higher Education
8701 Georgia Avenue
Silver Springs, MD 20910

Index